A SILENT MUSE

Jean Anne Watts

ARTHUR H. STOCKWELL LTD
Torrs Park, Ilfracombe, Devon, EX34 8BA
Established 1898
www.ahstockwell.co.uk

ISBN 978-0-7223-4309-8
Printed in Great Britain by
Arthur H. Stockwell Ltd
Torrs Park   Ilfracombe
Devon EX34 8BA

CONTENTS

ST PANCRAS

We see so much with new affection,
Since John Betjeman's direction.
A dulcet man whose lambent gaze
Delighted in our railway stations.
Those great and stately termini
With vast cathedral canopies
Of soaring vaulted ironwork,
In noble grandeur arced against the sky.
The stonework, the pilasters.
The dormers with their finials.
The charm of all the brick arcading –
even over modest doorways.
Impeccable in every detail,
Skill at every turn . . . the marvels of their age.
We had looked at them for ever,
But had never really seen them till
We looked again with his eyes
And knew that he was right.

A 'D' FROM THE ROYAL ACADEMY

The letter 'D' chalked on the back of your picture means
You didn't quite make it –
The line at the Royal Academy.
The picture was OK, indeed it was
Worthy of exhibition.
All the same it didn't quite make it.
But 'D' is a nice letter and seen
Sideways, and in the right light, and
If not chalked too well might almost be an 'A'
Even if it didn't quite make it.
So a 'D' should be treasured;
But, chalk being fugitive,
Better spray it with fixative
And hang it with the 'D' outside,
Which means the picture on the inside,
Though unheralded and unsung,
Very nearly did get hung.

A LEAF

A chestnut fan with six leaves or with seven –
Does it matter?
The cold uncounting wind will scatter all of them.
Be not concerned with numbers, be content;
A tree does not grow for argument.
If clarity of vision be so great,
To see so much is more than you can bear;
Half close your eyes and let the wonder there
Recede a little, just enough to see
The glory of this canopy, this tree.
Perception still will nourish your belief
In the greening, growing beauty of a leaf.

THE ADVENT BIRD

This haloed bird upon the bough
Kept watch the whole night through
As thou the Prince of Peace were born.

The same bird saw the Advent Star
Climb the Galilean sky,
Great light of love incarnate.

From branch to branch it followed
And, soaring, heard the angels sing
Of Thou, the Babe of virgin birth.

It came to rest among the men
Who watch were keeping of their sheep,
The angel of the Lord appearing –
Were they dreaming, half asleep?

It flew in at the open door,
Alighting softly on the floor, as Thou
Straw-mangered lowly lay, the Word made Flesh for us.

It came upon the maiden's hem
As ox and ass in patience stood,
First humbled, most knowing, pilgrims to Thy throne.

O little bird of Advent's eve,
Our Saviour's birth professing,
Make Joseph's staff thy resting place
And Mary's smile thy blessing.

MISSING

Still I seek you in the dark of night
And on the hill I hope to find you still.
Once I called you by your name,
And though I waited tense and pleadingly
No answer came nor hope had I –
Of even one more day.
Or, if an end a fading into age
And gentleness together,
Not this sudden plunging into a pit
Where I am lost for ever.

THE VISIT TO NORMANDY

Miss McIntyre,
You are wonderful.
The omelettes were divine
And the welcome that you gave us
Was absolutely fine.
I will always remember
The few hours spent with you,
Your warmth and friendly kindness,
The sheer great heartedness of you.
In a splintered, wounded country
In the days that followed war.
To all in search of comfort,
To all in need of aid,
Even those like us, just passing through –
An ever open door.
Yes, Miss McIntyre, you're a lady
And the omelettes were terrific.

TIGGER

Tigger, Tigger, Tigger cat,
Tawny tripod on the mat.
With flaring blaze of amber gaze,
O orange marmaladey cat.
Disabled with loss of single hip
You shift along the fence like a zip,
Or sit and bend your little head
To where you used to have a leg.
And stumpy shudders make it clear
You'd dearly love to scratch an ear.
I do it for you gladly and
You press your face into my hand,
With throbbing purrs of lyric note
From somewhere deep inside your throat.
Golden orbs go pupil black
As I make good the lack –
Ecstatic enigmatic slits
Say Tigger cat is thrilled to bits.

THE DRYSTONE WALLS OF WALES

Who made these cordons laid out sinew-strong?
Whose hands have placed these stones one upon another
To create mile on mile of undulating wall?
How many men have trod the early dawnings,
Boots swishing through the dewy grasses,
Legs all drenched with sturdy country strides.
What toil was theirs in girdling these high and empty places,
Embattled with the elements?
How meagre their reward?
God knows, who watched them labour so
Enclosing His creation.
A home of old this cottage derelict,
Thick-walled, blank-eyed and roofless to the sky.
Such men as these were born to days of poverty and labour,
Grew old upon the mountainside,
Unnamed, unnumbered, unremembered,
Yet their monuments endure.

MUSIC

Music is born in the ears of a child,
In the ears of a cornfield, in the wind running wild,
In the sibilant fall of a wave on the shore
Or the sigh of the sands as the waters withdraw.
The spheres in the heavens,
The rustle of leaves,
The movement of water in rivers and streams –
All these are, stave after stave, making music.
Why, the harmonic lyres of telegraph wires are music,
But chords above all;
The celestial wingbeats of swans as they fly,
Thrice blessed poem of sound in the sky,
Of the very best kind is their music.

PRAYER

Patience be my friend.
In grey times send
Peace into my heart and
Oh, a longer fuse
For temper's sake!
Lord, grant me this.

Patience be my friend.
So in my daily round or at my end,
Pain, confusion or despair
May be relieved by prayer.
Lord, grant me this.

POETRY IS . . .

A silent muse
Steals in upon my senses,
Unfolding bright assemblies
In my mind –
Of words – they come unbidden,
Clothing thoughts I did not summon
At a moment when
I had not planned to think.

CULLING GROUND

Strike out that word,
And that one.
The thought too far,
Too much.
The line too long,
All must go.
I am persuaded, it is clear
Poetry should be severe.

GUERNSEY HIGH SEAS

Three seas are met,
Three currents crossed.
And we unhappy souls are tossed
On swollen remnants of the storm
That swept these waters yesterday.
The sea is higher than the ship –
I close my eye as up we go.
I open them and there below
The seething, heaving ocean brew
Hasn't gone away.
Oh dear . . . sursum corda . . . at the rail
Is quicker, cleaner that a pail.

LOURDES

Lourdes is a difficult place to be if you are well.
It is too easy to be aloof from the suffering,
The raw emotion, the core of what it is all about;
Easy to recoil from the tawdry bazaar commerce –
Medals by the bucket, candles by the yard,
Statues that glow in the night.
Plastic Madonna holy-water bottles – oh dear!
The bell-hymn clamour of those incessant Aves –
Will they never end?

Lourdes swamps the senses, defeats language.
To write of it courts bathos,
But, but . . . in the stillness of the grotto,
In the flickering flare of candle prayer,
In the pain-wracked heart of it all
Is surely a source of grace,
So the dross of our lives is transformed
And all the right things fall into place.

So priest and nun, doctor, nurse
And all the sick pilgrims
Come quietly into their own.
Like a great homing of souls
In the mystery of faith.
Love is enough.

LANERCOST

We came to Carlisle from Arnside
In search of Hadrian's Wall.
We did not find it, but came instead
On something so surprising and so lovely –
Perhaps because we had not sought it –
Lanercost Priory.
There it stood in the full light of a midsummer's day,
And in the greenness of its setting,
Without even knowing the sweet reason for its being,
We were enchanted.
Augustinian, the book said, and founded by
William de Vaux in 1169.
Leaving alms with monks
To pray for the souls of parents,
Whilst he took the Cross and left
To crusade in the Holy Land

Lanercost, fair Lanercost.
Rose rising Lanercost,
Prayer bequest of filial gift,
This knightly gesture made thee.

WINTER, THEY SAY

Winter, they say,
Will clasp us all with icy hands
And iron-hard the earth will shrink from this embrace.
Bitter winds will pierce our lives
As cold insistent kissing snow,
Spreads a downy mantle over all.
The candour of its whiteness will amaze.
Its feather swirls will blur our sight.
Far and wide will scan our eyes
A land where no horizon lies.

A world of muffled purity,
That special hush of snow,
Where birds will soft exchanges make
And we will keep our voices low.
One with nature, just as though
A vast cathedral binds us all
To quietness and reverence
When winter's icy hands
Have clasped us so.

A WINTER'S TALE

Summer went in chastened glory.
Autumn too passed this way,
Its bright perfection burnishing the land.
And, following from branch to branch,
The wind has torn its harvest
From tree canopy, leaf sanctuary – all bare.
Naked bare, tree trunk spare,
Bark skeletons outstretch and lean
Into the bitter sky.
Imploring comfort from the stars
In lonely distant galaxies unfurled.
While, pendant-wise,
The moon's cold scimitar of light
Scarce casts a shadow on a sleeping world.
Sleep on, oh sleep –
This bitter night will etch such fantasies
As will astound our morning dullard eyes.
A single diadem of frost upon a leaf,
A fresco of such symmetry
Upon a windowpane
Will so enchant a child's awakened sight.
But tremulously traced and steamed away,
What wide-eyed sorrow will erase
The joy of this discovery?

CAMUSDARACH BAY

Shell opalescent pink
The sands of Camusdarach Bay.
As I gaze upon their billow dunes
Beside the gentle sea,
A roseate skein of colour with
A pale and tender sheen and
A softness like no other sands
That I have ever seen.
What other wordly paradise
To crest a slope and see?
Shell opalescent pink
The sands of Camusdarach be.

BENDERLOCH

In Scotland
The weather was not fine,
But, fleetingly,
The cloudy carapace rose from the heights
So azure-lined, their profiles were unrolled.
And there the snows of May were still unmelted
In gully scree and granite outcrop's hold.

But still –
The weather is not fine,
So fleetingly capricious as a dream upon a brow,
Regretfully, the misty veil descending.
Silence sighs to rest about us now.

PONT D'ESPAGNE, 1973

The road to Pont d'Espagne is like this:
At some times of the day you go up,
At other times you can come down;
At no time of the day can you do both. It's like that.

When we went up a storm raged round the coach all the way.
Thunder crashing, lightning flashing, rain lashing,
Violent and frightening.
At the top the storm had spent itself and
All was quiet, calm and beautiful.
I sat trailing my feet in rock-cleft pool,
Flinching from its icy swirl, and
Watched water hurtling in torrents from high above,
Sheeting from rock to rock with huge force.
Diamond spray rainbowing in the clear sky – magic.
Pont d'Espagne in the High Pyrenees.

TODAY

The past is gone –
What lies ahead we cannot know,
Or stay its coming.
Only this moment is within grasp
And I within the circle of your arms,
Am happy for it to be so,
Without regrets or questioning
The always of my love for you,
Or yours for me.
For always is the sand from glass
To glass arrested in its flight,
Or wild delight of hands,
However tightly laced.
Glad spirits to each other flown.

SUNDAY PAPER

Yes, yes, we've got it.
You push, we will pull;
That's it – just another tug
And now we have it all.
Right, now everyone has a piece.
Dad, the sports section;
Eldest boy, the motor-show supplement;
Another has the coloured bit;
And baby, the business section – upside down.
At two? Such judgement – how splendid!
I say, why don't we open the door
And let the poor lad hand the paper to us –
One week,
When the Sunday paper is icumen in?

WHILE YOU WAIT

The funniest ad I ever read
Was in the local paper.
It said,
'Ears pierced while you wait.'

And if you don't wait, there is another way?